REMARKABLE OCCURRENCES

by the same author

AN ANNIVERSARY OF FLIGHT
SHENANIGANS

Remarkable Occurrences

Patrick Lodge

Valley Press

First published in 2019 by Valley Press
Woodend, The Crescent, Scarborough, YO11 2PW
www.valleypressuk.com

First edition, first printing (July 2019)

ISBN 978-1-912436-27-9
Cat. no. VP0147

Copyright © Patrick Lodge 2019

The right of Patrick Lodge to be identified as the
author of this work has been asserted in accordance with
the Copyright, Designs and Patents Act 1988.

All rights reserved. No part of this publication may be
reproduced, stored in or introduced into a retrieval system,
or transmitted in any form, by any means (electronic,
mechanical, photocopying, recording or otherwise) without
prior written permission from the rights holders.

A CIP record for this book is available from the British Library.

Cover illustration © National Maritime Museum, Greenwich, London.
Cover and text design by Jamie McGarry.

Printed and bound in Great Britain by
Imprint Digital, Upton Pyne, Exeter.

Contents

The Log Delivery   11
Ynys Enlli   12
Deux Soeurs   13
The Volta Cinematograph   14
On Onasagorou Street   15
Supper at Plas-Yn-Rhiw   17
What Remained   18
Agios Ioannis O Makra Talaporia   19
Red Thread   21
Vernal Equinox   23
Sunrise Swim   24
Legendary Knitting   25
Anaiya   26
On a Boat with Scully   27
The Politically Incorrect Duck   28
Orkney: Four Mini Sagas   29
Pintando Todo El Dia   31
Purusha   32
wonderland   33
Eastern Ghouta   34
Sleeping with Dylan Thomas   35
Panegyric for Cardiff Mods   36
The Greatest of These   37
Light Up, Caravaggio   38
In an Amount Sufficient to Cause Death   40
The Kite and the Fool Take the Air   41
The Fifth Morning   42
Ar Llwybr Arfordir Cymru   43
Hic Omnia Remedia   44
Ballerina Bride   45
A Fisherman at Laolongtou   46

Null-Acht-Fünfzehn   47
The Dustbin of History   48
Saturday Market, Rahovec, Kosovo   49
Late Afternoon, Prince Consort Gardens   50
Notes to Part One   53

REMARKABLE OCCURRENCES

Song of Whitby   57
Song of the Endeavour   58
Song of George Dorlton   59
Song of the Young Sailor   60
Song of William Greenslade, Marine   62
Song of Joseph Banks   63
Song of Tupaia   65
Song of Young Nick   68
Song of the Kauri Trees   69
Song of the First Contact   72
Song of Sydney Parkinson   79
Song of the Tupapaku   81
Song of the Cannibalism   82
Song of the Severed Head   83
The Song of Possession   84
Song of the Leaving   85
Song of Botany Bay   87
Song of the Bitch, Lady   90
Song of Celebrity   91
Notes to Remarkable Occurences   95

Acknowledgements

I am grateful to the editors of the following magazines and anthologies where versions of some of these poems first appeared: *The High Window*, *As Above So Below*, *Boyne Berries*, *Dreamcatcher*, *Setu*, *The Bees Breakfast* (Beautiful Dragons), *Not A Drop* (Beautiful Dragons), *Watch the Birdie* (Beautiful Dragons), *Poems For Cardiff* (Seren).

'Song of The Endeavour' was performed at the 2017 Leeds Lieder Festival with accompanying music by Jay Platt.

'wonderland' was shortlisted for the 2018 Leeds Poetry Peace Prize.

Five of the poems herein were commended in the 2018 Gregory O'Donoghue Poetry Competition.

'Eastern Ghouta' was shortlisted for the Trim Poetry Festival Competition, 2019.

'Vernal Equinox' was shortlisted for the Poetry On The Lake competition, 2019

'On A Boat With Scully' won the Blackwater International/Red House Poets Poetry Competition, 2019

*To my Grandchildren
Poppy, Dexter, Isobella, Anaiya
in hope that they can sort out the mess
we left for them*

'Give me your hand
get lost with me.
Give me your hand,
can't you see what we'll meet,
where no-one,
no-one else has been.
No passengers,
travel as pilots,
come, my raging fantasy.'

Amelia Earhart

Lyrics by Marilena Zacheos
Performed by Grendel Babies
on the album *Oh My!*

'The traveller takes himself wherever he goes'
– Montaigne

The Log Delivery

Bowie blaring from the truck cab.
The deliveryman is a cool dancer;
sashaying outrageously, he manhandles
the bulk bags from flat-bed to drive.

Wood warms three times, he says:
once when you cut it,
once when you stack it,
once when you burn it.

That is true but there's more.
Before a fire is laid, a log fetched in,
the sufficiency of a packed log pile
is warming enough, solstice looming.

Here are deeper timbres working:
it's primal, this sense of each log
added to the stack as an amulet
against winter's continuing snubs.

Every one hoards the heat of summers
gone. All are enthusiasts, radiant
as a struck match flaring for its rebel
moment, incandescent against shadows.

But after that the end is always ash,
a cold darkness as yet unimagined.

Put another log on the fire for me…

Ynys Enlli

(Bardsey Island)

We bounce across on sunlight slivers
from Porth Meudwy to Ynys Enlli,
flying over shoals and rips, tide-racing
like arrows homing to a martyr's side.

On this island of pilgrims, every step
taken is to hear underfoot the crunch
of saints' bones; to lie outstretched
on grass is to be measured up for eternity.

They've been in that business here for ever.
Peel the stratified mélange of sanctities,
it's Bronze Age cremation ash at the base
binding the mortar of all foundations.

Celt, Catholic, Pagan – all found themselves
became solitaries, wrestling with hermeneutics,
walking and praying over God's square mile,
bent low, the wind howling everything easterly.

Impossible not to be altered even in a few hours.
Everyone sloughs off something – leaves it
laid down like sedimentary rock – a deposit
of eremitic faith for all who follow to feed on.

Homeward on the bright twin-engined sarcophagus,
all seem lightened; yet some have pocketed shells
and all will carry ballast from this island,
something of the spirit, something for the journey.

Deux Soeurs

A year apart, two sisters
one a spinster, the other
still shrugging her way
into the solaces of a new
surname, have their deaths
incised on grey stone.

Hard granite it looks,
propped in a recess
of a barn with outline
permissions. Not hard
enough to defy the axe
that cracked it sideways.

One blow, parting forever
two women torn apart in life
by the man who paid
for everything other than
this gravestone, gracing
neither grave, nor memory.

The Volta Cinematograph

Another piss into the chamber pot
tinkles its pretty music to eternity
and makes me no richer, no wiser.
Here was the conundrum: Trieste,
full of cinemas; Dublin, not a one,
and me puffed as the first tycoon,
Ireland's bright cinematographic star.
I owed the sisters something but this work!
Am I a writer or a Mr. Ten Percent?
A ghost of myself? A mere lapwing?
Sandwiched and bored,
between Scylla and Charybdis, I am
a wanderer wandering, a hesitating soul
always seeking out adventures.
Here's a proverb for our time:
a bicycle shop owner and other foolsheads
do not a picturehouse empire make.
James Joyce is not to be the Dublin mogul,
though a man of genius makes no mistakes.
I'd rather swallow a crab than admit
nothing can be done here,
that once again my city failed me,
has scarred my heart with its name.
Time for a quick about turn – lead me forward!
Life will become art! I will be a hero!
Chamber music… Chamber music…
Could make a kind of pun on that
diddleiddle addleaddle oodleoodle…

On Onasagorou Street

For a few days in Spring
I may steal the sun's first
heat. I will take a room
on Onasagorou Street.
You may remember
the hotel; it is small
and will prove discrete.
I always book the Green Room
(a favourite, I think?);
it is comfortable
if there is waiting or, if
there is not. Either way.
In the mornings you can
find me at a café nearby –
a shisha, a fresh lemonade.
Maybe it will be appropriate
then to take that walk
to Eleftherias and back.
Always the same route;
these may become rituals,
and could be important.
Afternoons, I hope to relax
on the balcony where
I may smoke a cigarette.
Looking up from the street,
there are the green shutters,
the familiar iron scroll-work.
You would know it, I am sure.
Should there be a delay
for a day or two, I won't worry.
There's always an exhibition
at the Leventis to occupy
me while I wait.

It will be sometime since
we last met (do you remember
the promises of that last night?
You looked pale, were deathly
quiet, still as the grave).
I haven't changed much –
you'd know me instantly.
I took your smile for safe-
keeping, you will recognise it
shining brightly through me.

Supper at Plas-Yn-Rhiw

("there is no death while memory lives")

The three sisters Keating lay for supper
their blue and white Alfred Meakin china.
Four places? – possibly a land agent, a local
poet or just a ritual of hospitality and hope.
The paraffin range will burn bright tonight,
the produce of the kitchen garden, steam. Later
the Home Service, maybe the phonograph will
play light classics – the Laughing Policeman
is ready should some fun be required.
In the end the light will dim, the blood-red
geraniums at the window shrink to black.
Each sister to their bed, past the rack
of dusty fashionable shoes, Slade-inspired
landscapes by Honora and friends. One
sister will regress under a child's patchwork
quilt, read of three bright girls in faded gentility.
She may look up from the narrow bed
see again, in the moon light over the Llyn,
the armoured knight forever failing
to free the distrait lady from the binding tree.

What Remained

All the flight I watched your smile
even at take-off when all is suspenseful   contingent
when past and present
mock each other's pretensions
of confidence

I looked at your eyes too
they were deeper than Lethe
never chill   but
I could not forget anything

Certainly not the women who looked like you
                              on the vineyard roof close to the brink

    the women who held hands to dance in circles
                          to the cliff edge
                  singing for themselves alone
                      in love not desperation
                whose eyes though were dead
      whose smiles were fixed for a worse world

who placed their hopes
only in the sustaining lightness of air
like that air which held a tiny cloud
far below the plane   so lost   between sky and parched earth
that I had to stare hard past the wing into the vivid sun
flooding the world with carmine lullabies
so as not to cry for it   and

for what remained
so light   so light it could not
be kept hold of   arms had tried as if it was heavy and dense
and must   like love eventually
be free

Agios Ioannis O Makra Talaporia

It is an Ionian wind
brought by a sky
so blue, so transparent,
that to conjecture cloud
would be an apostasy.
It brings layers
of warm herbs –
oregano, thyme, basil –
the bake of hot sand,
of hot skin, of promise.

It brings Piz Buin too,
from the Greeks
on the adjacent sunbeds
whose classical profiles,
coruscating hair,
heroic poses with Frisbee
and beach bat,
channel the spirit
of this place

better than the Attic
antics on the mini-market
tourist-tat pottery.
Etched in black
on red clay, furtive
sunset shadows
appear to couple (and more)
to the limits of ingenuity,
of flexibility. Racked
promiscuously
on pine shelves,
they are a window to the mythic,
a high-octane romp
of Olympian proportions

but still, they set me dreaming…
whitewashed cubes
hanging off the slope
to the bay, bougainvillea,
a forensic spatter of bougainvillea
around the door,
window frames so many attempts
at blue, as if a painter
with no words,
compulsively sought
to speak of the sea
through them
shimmering heat
making unreliable witness
to everything beyond
these shuttered, cave-dark rooms,
parched by unmoved, imprisoned air
furnished like hermit cells
smelling of sex and sweet resin
almost sacred
cicadas
the serpent hiss
of an old fridge cooling wine,
tangled sheets,
discarded pillows
what shades have exchanged
themselves here
what shades might still…

The wind drops,
the corset heat clamps tight to the bones.
A single bell tolls from the tower
of Agios Ioannis O Makra Talaporia.
There may be storms tonight;
there is hope of lightning.

Red Thread

This morning I passed
high over Ireland;
at thirty thousand feet
according to the pilot –
a man with an accent
scrambled by living
too long under the moon –
whose words interrupt
the *hare rama* looping
through my headphones.

Over County Cork, I think,
the cloud cover dispersed;
townlands, bogs, fields,
clumped houses, throwing
shadows like serried graves,
came into still, silent focus.
I swear I saw a red thread
coiling over crossroads,
fields and burial grounds,
in and out of front doors,

around crosses, monastic
ruins, famine cottages,
uprising statues, bars
speaking my lost name,
with their back rooms full
and their front ones too.
Knotting known ankles,
unknown too – fraught,
yet however tightly tied,
not snapping until it must.

Intuitively, my arms raise
as they did for my mother,
in nightshade exile, who spun
wool, black as shiny berry,
to a ball from the hank, I held,
who made something of it.
Cloud thickens again, the world
below obscures. We start
our descent to the end
of the trip: all is unturnable.

Vernal Equinox

I swear I saw

the spirit of the hare
festal
in the half of night that now becomes day
rise up

from the bloodshot tarmac
from the blatant bones
from the visceral forfeit

gather in
complete and lithe
ears raised
nose twitching
eyes seeing clear
unmoving for a moment
then springing aloft

transparent
unbroken
faultless

ascending through air
to fire
that consumes breath itself
an ardent thread
a filament
that shone in the firmament
embossed above
a light alone
pure

I saw I swear

Sunrise Swim

At dawn the pool is bereft,
its surface, a mirror, reflecting
endless air leaking
into space; a balsam breeze
through the olive trees – heavy
with the spoor of honey-pot

herb fields stretching away
to the black-pine Mount Aenos –
is all that disturbs its core.
The sun rises through cypress
stands, fingers of shade
reaching for the poolside

but I'm leading the measure,
quickly into a metronomic
swim, swinging arms keeping
the beat until… time stops;
three swifts, in line next to me,
drop to scoop a beak of water.

I'm caught mid-stroke,
crooked arm high in the air,
head tilted to catch a breath,
to catch the lead bird's sip.
An extraordinary, consecrated
moment that I nag for insight.

Until it dawns on me that
if a camera froze that image
of pool, swimmer, bird, distilled
that perfect instant to a chrism,
I would have it as an anointing
worthy for a final crossing.

Legendary Knitting

(for Anaiya Rose Blades)

Cast on…

All winter you hunched fetal,
leaning into scraps of light
leaking through windows,
apologising from eco-bulbs,
eyes cat-slitted in focus.
Friends came by, randomly
offered a line, dropped stitches
over scandi-noir and red wine.
The needles burred, whispered
of love and hope above
a purr of memories and yarns.
Inch by inch it developed,
unfurled for review a neutral
palette: an ensign, a pennant,
finally a fully-fledged flag
of a country undiscovered,
that no explorer has seen,
whose borders, secured at last,
gather up the precious produce.
Now is the time of legend,
nail your colours to the mast,
get shipshape, get on board.

Cast off…

Anaiya

How is it that this joyous beginning
encourages thoughts of endings?
Inevitable, I suppose; holding you
in two clumsy hands, only hours old,
post-partum perfection emerging,
it seems stages of this tour
are completing, boxes being ticked,
batons being passed on.
Though the clichés are a loose fit. Naked
you may have come into this world
but never alone; as for me,
I'll take my leave in old pajamas
or a baggy hospital gown, knowing less
than you do now and who knows
what draw I'll be at the final curtain.
Here's me slowing down, humping
the debris of decades. They were right,
it's a drag; but you, from that first
slick slide into the light, into your becoming,
can only accelerate from here –
a million neural connections a second
sparking crosses in this synaptic bingo game.
Your mouth already an O of wonder;
your eyes, perfect sky, limitless,
going in and out of focus
looking for clues, then suddenly
staring, like it could, after all, make sense.

Here, let me look in my pack, find
my best day of the twenty-five thousand
odd I've managed to lose someplace.
You can have it, a gift… something to start with.

On a Boat with Scully

*I want to remember
how it all was.*
I sat with Scully
on a boat without oars,
tethered to the jetty –
a shroud-laid umbilical
reefed to the world.
We argued.
(She'd been here before).
*Loosen that knot, you'll
never get back to the shore.*
I caught her drift;
but maybe there are
no choices to be made,
no signs to point a way?

The lake was deadpan;
a breath would barely fog
the mirror calm.
I don't see Scully now
but I want to believe,
except it's all unraveling,
as a strand looses the tide
I'm unremembering all
those moments which coasted me
to this boat, on this lake.
Eyes closed,
opening only once to look –
that's where I've been all this time.
Reach for the rope, let's go;
out there? *out there!*

The Politically Incorrect Duck

(Clangula hyemalis)

There was enough to bother about
before the committee stuck their beak in.
What with the pollution, the learning
to fly underwater (I'm the only one
that can do it – clocked at 60 metres!),
the finding somewhere to overwinter –
(cold, but not Baltic enough to freeze
my feathers to the bone). Now, to top it all,
the AOU (who they? I squawk) have fully
plucked me. Changed my name. I am now
(deep breath) the long tailed duck, ta ra!
Let's all be clear, I'm still a ruddy duck!
A duck is a duck is a duck,
as Gertrude Stein almost wrote.
I have a long tail, I am a duck:
ergo – I am a long-tailed duck. Fair dos.
Not that I liked my previous moniker.
Oldsquaw? I can see where it came from –
jovial is my middle name, I do like to chat –
little else to do in a pond with your mates.
But I get on swimmingly with the tribes;
they've even been helping conserve me.
So goodbye to a nickname that touches
all bases of prejudice. Sexist, racist, ageist –
whatever, duck and its hoary handle are parted.
Oldsquaw is no more and good riddance:
time for a callithumpian quacking celebration!

Orkney: Four Mini Sagas

("firgive vus sinna vora" – part of the Lord's Prayer in Norn)

No 1 Broughton

It's a scream; that
here is where it starts.
Bluish shutters, salty,
wind-worried;
slats askew,
so that the sun
scratches a shadow ladder
only halfway up a wall;
no climb out of the hole from here.
Raise your eyebrows,
see it clearly –
skull, blood, bones.
We can't escape.

On the Low Road

Driving from Isbister
at noon,
I see oystercatchers
probe for shellfish
but snub
the gull settled on the low road.
It rose from the tarmac,
was held spread-eagled in a crosswind,
like a totem image,
until the car's impact
defleshed it,
disarticulated
the intricate bone structure,
gravely laid it aside.

Hamnavoe

Going home peaceful
from the Ferry Inn;
a cobbled carriage-track
curves away
glistening wet after rain.
It catches the sunset,
becomes a shimmering, swaying
path to somewhere else
that breaks apart as I walk it.
A piper starts up
with *Cumha na Cloinne,*
the drone bringing
me back to earth.

Pierowall

Dawn. From the window,
a rainbow selects
Freya's house
across the bay.
Fortunate people, sleeping
under a feather cover,
dream of transfiguration,
half their souls already lost.
A seal snouts seaweed rafts,
settling as the water recedes.
The fire hots up here;
Freya cries bloodshot tears,
but stays cool.

Pintando Todo El Dia

(i.m. César Manrique)

Painting all day, it says;
the diary has blank page
after blank, lined page.
Each one has day, month,
date – other distractions too,
holydays and holidays.

These impositions meant
little; you dismissed them
with that careful script –
pintando todos el dia.

What else was there to do
except save an island
from itself, save a world
from negotiating the future
of every creature, every
landscape on the basis
of the bottom line.

It's over now: clocks tick
over the celebrity photos,
vinyl waits for a needle drop,
brushes stiffen under
the last canvasses.

Tranquil
at the Casa Manrique;
you can lie back,
turn inside out,
exhale,
dream.

Purusha

Three scents you gave me:

first,
on your cupped palms,
burning with cinnamon oil,
held as if exposing wounds to doubters;

second,
your perfume on my skin
until the sea burnished me
in the morning light;

third,
a stub of temple incense,
broken, each half lit at an understood
but unspoken moment.

This I recall, but here's the sense:
how, kneading muscles, working bones,
you made me formless, shapeless,
then built a perfect space,
a womb house,
where all that is essence quickens.

wonderland

Mist swaddles the roofs. Paths glint, slick
and greasy; take-away cartons drift into kerbs.
Streetlights struggle. It could be a grimupnorth
Grimshaw scene but this is Leeds, Christmas 2017.
In Victoria Square a gaudy fairground
celebrates with children's rides, candy floss,
bright plastic novelties from the east.
A temporary PA thumps out seasonal songs
of plenty on a loop; ironic or sentimental
they are remorseless in their frenzy of cheer.
Nobody is dancing in the Valhalla Bar.
A man does the rounds of wisecracking drinkers,
tries to beg a pound for a burger and fries,
says he hasn't eaten for a few days. No-one
disbelieves him, no-one gives him a coin.
Others stand by the doorway neither in nor out;
holding bedrolls, holding dogs on a string,
shuffling from foot to foot. They wait
for something to happen as if roughing it
on a bleak hillside somewhere, sometime.
They wait for the angels at the shelter
to open up; they can taste the stew already.
Two teenage girls pass by. One pushes
a pushchair, her festive headband wobbles;
a star blinks wanly, the other is lost forever.
I can't get into Christmas no more, she says.
Her friend wears a stained T-shirt, "wonderland"
in fierce day-glo fights the gloom. *No,* she says,
It's all crap and the food bank had no chipolatas.
Floating above it all, on a poppy-wreathed plinth
a marble column holds up a seraph. All thoughts
of victory lost, she has put down her sword
holds out to her city a single rose, in memory of love.

Eastern Ghouta

She dusts off the wooden box
her mother gave
in another life. A star
emerges in cellar gloom.
Interlaced strips of dreams
seen now only in veneers:
peach, apricot, walnut, rose.
Inlaid is nacre, lustrous
as evening-brushed hair.
*Look at this, daughter,
and be calmed,* she said,
on that special day.

She opens the box,
takes out a lipstick,
a shard of glass
from her grandmother's
mirror that had hung
for ever in the hall.
Carefully she paints
her mouth; rose-lipped wife,
her husband smiled once.
If he does not return
and the soldiers come
she will use the glass…

she will bloom again.

Sleeping with Dylan Thomas

The bed is too narrow; it will squeak,
I know it will, metal on metal, grinding.
The pillowslips look nicotine-stained.

The room stinks of Woodbines. I'd open
a window but it lets the seaweed in;
I can't appear half-drowned on my debut.

The curtains are closed; the view
leaves much to be desired anyway.
I would always favour my mind's eye.

I wait, spelling words with used matches.
Auden, Eliot, Yeats ogle from the walls;
Pamela's there too, mumbling in her tight shorts.

He could be in the bath; I've already been
there – a quick in and out, just a peek.
The pipes bang and groan as if in ecstasy.

He would be in all night if he felt like it.
Books, and boiled sweets lined up to suck.
Not my idea of a steamy date.

I've closed the door but nothing gets larger,
not even the possibilities. Time to make
my apologies and go. Roger and out.

Panegyric for Cardiff Mods

White boys on the weekend searching for their soul;
sta-prest, back-combed, pilgrims at the Top Rank Suite.
It's the 60s man; see them dance, losing control.

Rondella, the Face, puppet master at the console,
loads the 45s, pulls the strings that jerk loafered feet.
White boys on the weekend searching for their soul

to the liturgy of Stax, like postulants, shoal
close to the girls radiating risk, pubescent heat.
It's the 60s man; see them dance, losing control.

In the spots the dance floor is a goldfish bowl,
a land of a thousand dancers, steadfast in the beat.
White boys on the weekend searching for their soul,

an exodus from the suburbs, needing to become whole;
staunch as neophytes, they suck fierce on the music's teat.
It's the 60s man; see them dance, losing control

Fast forward fifty years, the faith remains whole;
a recalled underground life, transfigured and complete.
White boys on the weekend searching for their soul.
It's the 60s man; see them dance, losing control.

The Greatest of These

(York Minster, Summer 2017)

A couple came out of the darkness
under the arch; chatting non-stop,
maybe flirting. The great East Window,
scaffold-free, transfigured in the sun.
Without a pause in the chit-chat,
as if compelled, one raised a phone,
like an oblation, clicked off a shot.
I was dismissive; how could pixels
comprehend the moment she was in;

a stockpiled image was no substitute
for her being there, completed, true,
senses, spirit, soul as one. Then,
the ultimate cliché, a gurning
selfie against the soaring cathedral.
But as she leaned back, the better
to frame gargoyle or saint, balance
was lost and intuitively her escort
steadied her with a hand to the back.

There was the beginning and end of it;
an act of almost sexual choreography
carrying such a sensation of love,
such intimations of profound intimacy,
that all who witnessed must be humbled.
They walked on past my café table,
laughing and arms linked, in step,
so close they must seem to each other
to be holding on to themselves.

Light Up, Caravaggio

(Cesari Chapel, Santa Maria del Popolo, Roma)

Light up Caravaggio,
the sign on the brass box tempts.
Wanderers ghostly in their gloom
wait for the first to crack.
A tourist drops a euro in the slot;
the world becomes fluorescent
as if lightning had struck –
for a few minutes we are actors
aghast in saintly altar visions.

Paul, like us, falls flat on his way
to righteousness. The world's a horse's arse,
blocking the divine light that poked
out his eyes. He's shafted; no reason in it.
Perhaps Peter thought it through, though
his world's spun topsy-turvy – a euro's
worth of radiance proves a shocker.
He blinks, as if just noticing his nailed palm,
the sweaty efforts to exalt soles heavenward.

And the painter – exposed to acres of holy
canvas, but still at heart, leaden,
a saturnalian. Lit up in brothels,
dressed to kill, swinging sex like a sword,
he clubbed light into corners
the better to shadow his own virile misery.
Burning the candle at both ends,
until bad blood and the bright sun
spiked him in some Tuscan hole.

At least he sucked it up while he could;
deny it as many times as you like,
but, at a stretch, we're all bound
to walk that walk, like it or not.
Clockwork ticks on; brilliance dims.
Clink! The coin falls, the chapel recedes.
Unaltered souls, we're out of this prison
of devout darkness sharpish.
Time to hit the bars; time to lighten up.

In an Amount Sufficient to Cause Death

My end is a higher education in metallurgy;
a first degree in the mechanics of killing.
The strap-down team arrives to execute a suave
totentanz; I am gurneyed, burnished buckles

clack shut, splay my arms tight to this chrome
crucifix. I am a nailed-on certainty to die today.
The thrumming of tin cups on iron bars –
an unalloyed percussion of death – is my threnody

as I am delivered from a windowless room
to a star-shell sparkling chamber exploding
with yellow mercury light. This is a ferrous
domain; a buffed, stainless, sterile cube

where ceiling reflects floor reflecting ceiling.
An infinity of mirrors in which I diminish.
Alchemists hook me up, I am become cyborg,
pierced by shiny steel needles like little reeds

that will pipe a lament into my bloodstream
at the plunge of the hard-tempered syringe.
I know the protocol – I exchange fluids
with the machine. First, the seep of sedation comes:

second, the spreading stain of paralysis.
I am a driverless car racing nowhere.
My brain goes molten; I cannot think straight.
I am careening in the dark. I shout silently.

Thirdly, the potassium gift is given and sparks
through my veins like ore in the mother lode.
I am smelted pure but stay heavy, can't rise above it.
I am transfigured. This is glorious light. Full stop.

The Kite and the Fool Take the Air

Framed in the flaking casement,
twenty feet away from the fool
as the crow flies, the kite hovers,
windblown, vagrant in his element
as if an air-born archangel.

His wingtips twitch contempt
for the tug of the unfurled
valley below. Kite imagines
all beneath in stasis and scurry;
looks for the warm scuttle
or the scandal of cold death.
He is no healer.

Kite has faith in the buoyant rush
of unseen air; his is sky breath,
intense and tearing.
Rufous, yellow-clawed kite,
a hooded ember puffed
into glowing glead by the rush
of oxygen over wing,
descends like a yellow dagger.

The feather-headed fool watches;
whistles a melodious tune,
conducts himself as if with a wand.
His mien is cheerful, untrammelled.
One step over the sill; if he
invokes the keen moorland air
the aether will uphold him.

Fool can become kite and soar.
He puffs out his breast like a keel,
flaps his arms, slips through
the open window to a new beginning.

The Fifth Morning

We played tanks that evening,
my temperature may have peaked.
We played tanks in the fever-rich
bed surrendered by my parents.

You drove, I was the gunner.
Sometimes you were Dan Dare
and I was Flamer – the Mekon
took a pasting not the Hun.

Four days helpless, all innocent,
though I helped everyone understand.
The fifth morning my legs betrayed me;
from the floor I could see the future.

Ar Llwybr Arfordir Cymru

The weather app looks bleak
but an inner sun warms me.
My boots know my feet; they
know the path that splits sea
from land, that curls serpentine

over ragged, bitten borderlines.
I take in my stride this Brythonic
landscape, where each step murmurs
gofalwch wraig, mae pergyl yma.
But here is succour: I will respect

the dragon shell. Pilgrim fierce,
in squall or spate, one pace follows
another, there and back again
until my white barn, tethered
between land and sky, coddles me

with burning logs, steaming bath.
On a plain table lies all else:
one pencil, one pure paper sheet
where I must write the seal's bark,
the salt spray savour, the kelp reek.

Hic Omnia Remedia

(Nuestra Senora de los Remedios, Haria)

In this sacred space, against the priest's
mumbled ritual, a small congregation
stifles and shuffles until the holy fools
explode into the nave. All look as if dressed
in the dark from someone else's wardrobe;
a few chain-smoke unlit cigarettes. Here are
the least of the brethren: wheel-chaired,
zimmer-framed, bewildered. A saintly chaos
whose eyes flick from side to side,
at once feral and fearful; they take all in
and let it out like exhaling a final breath.

Their nurses are immaculate: young women,
marble jailer-madonnas, who self-consciously
shape pietàs pushing their charges into pews.
But one escapes, an elderly lady, dressed
impeccably, in clothes fashionable enough
for a 1950s wedding, makes it to the altar,
pushing the priest aside. Half the saints wake
as she stands stork-like, pointing up
sermonizing about piety, duty. More hear the call
and follow. They are children, upending tables,
spilling leaflets; a bentwood chair cracks like a whip.

But the carer hounds are quick, the flock herded
out to the sunbaked plaza, onto a mini-bus.
The righteous breathe a sigh of relief, settle again.
The priest looks heavenwards, *"comencemos de nuevo?"*
There may be no other way.

Ballerina Bride

(for AGB, 03/06/16)

Ballerina bride,
en pointe on red soles,
I walked with you
into an unfolding choreography
that was always your story.
This was your dance,
the steps fluid but precise;
your steps.

A few simple phrases
repeated
transmuted everything.
You were spirit, aerial,
danced free of all that was past.
Transformed in light
you were amazing,
you were grace.

A Fisherman at Laolongtou

A ten thousand mile long, earth-bound dragon
journeys to dip an old head into the sea of Bo;
drinks deeply, as if *tong sui* might brim the flagon.

But no sweet water delights, all taste in escrow
since dragon's descendants struck oil and gas
to power another leap forward above the guano.

Sea lanes etch the gulf's surface; black glass,
scored deep by the rough diamond of progress,
it traps exhausted species in a sterile casque.

A fisherman hauls in empty nets with a noblesse
only ancestors, who strode waves, might fathom.
No-one will follow. His child, drawn to city excess,

chased a different dragon; floater in a Beijing slum,
he nods and drops a fiery pearl, hope a phantom.

Null-Acht-Fünfzehn

(for the Leeds Pals, written July 1 2018)

forward   *feed*   *back*
tack   *tack*   *tack*

bullets with dumb logic
stammer across the broken field
each leaves a momentary hush
in its wake a million pauses
in the chatter of a morning's killing
stitch these seconds together
to quilt an undying conversation

for the tongue-tied pals
called out that morning from trenches
to lie down in a memory of quiet meadows
comfortable in themselves
like parting lovers
who don't need to say anything
in the short time left to them as whole

these cloth-eared evangelists
who once heard the brassy call
though some may conjure a lark singing
now strain with shell-dumb ears
to hear a whistle jab the tranquility
they stand up adjust themselves
and as if stepping out for a modest stroll

jag forward into 0.12 seconds of silence
wherein lay all that remains to them
until remembrance returns these soldiers
to village and town when smiling
they might wander among us gathered
wondering at what we have become
at how well we have used their gift

The Dustbin of History

A wheelie-bin, top flipped
open, spills the beans:
a ClearSign test kit,
(*two sticks still foiled*);
a ten pack of Blue Royals,
(*in this context "smoking kills"
seems oddly hopeful*);
a half bottle, own-brand gin,
(*cap off, lip-sticked mouth*).

What small dramas
these accidental forensics insinuate.
More soap opera than CSI –
that roaring night last week
with too many lacunae for comfort?
That budding relationship
promising everything until texts
bounced back unread?
All now in the dustbin of history.

But here's the catch –
such scripts amount to zilch.
Life's always an arrangement
of arbitrary evidence,
compacted, squeezed, distorted;
any logic only when seen backlit
or when the credits
begin to roll.

Close the lid, pass on by, smile.

Saturday Market, Rahovec, Kosovo

The adhan breaks the darkness across a valley
studded with lit minarets like rockets to God.
Traders don't wait for dawn – there are cities to be built,
economies to fashion from cardboard, offcuts, junk;
whatever falls to hand these country builders use.

The sun rises over mountains of fruit, vegetables –
a Balkan cornucopia, food enough to feed a nation.
Someone sprays a tray of small fish, water from a cola
bottle, a baptism of hope. Another buys two chickens,
frees them from a coop, dangles them home to pot.

Here is a history of clothing, an exhibition open to all
with last decade's colour, camouflage – gilets,
shemags, combat jackets and pants, still in vogue
on the brutalist statues and memorials scattered
in the countryside. All sloughed off here, recycled.

Next, all you could need to rebuild anything, anywhere.
Tractor parts, gearboxes, recovered nails and screws,
Chinese tools, auto salvage, appliances needing repair,
pieces of metal or plastic whose origins are mysterious.
Stalls fit for a nation of renovators with a job to be done.

Nothing is marked up yet everything has its price,
teased out by the sibilant hagglers after deals.
A coffee-drinking, chain-smoking, qeleshe-wearing
parliament of buyers and sellers, fixers and chancers
keeping the wheels turning on the road, their way.

Late Afternoon, Prince Consort Gardens

A squad of empty benches
stares seaward, ghostly defenders
watching for an invasion.
Tarnished plaques,
pinned to slats as if to veterans'
lapels, evoke
the dedicatees. Recalled
by nickname or diminutives,
any gravity offered by death, adrift.

Marching past, I speak names
out loud to the empty park;
a survivors' roll call, except,
in this park of the dead, they are not.
I improvise a cadence with their eulogies:
who loved this place very much
who couldn't get enough of this view
who gave his all to this town
who worked for others till the end.

Sad valedictions to the loyal and true;
as final as the bracketed dates
that forever follow close behind.
Now they keep themselves
to themselves, but keep company
with the view – skyward
across Steep Holm, a silvered
shining promissory pathway,
where some here once saw hope.

More solace than the adulterers
waiting in their cars for the light to fade,
to memorialize their lusts.
Or than the two lines of slithering
sulfur mustard pollution, outflanking
power station and factory stack
to rally above the gardens. Outriders
of the looming storm, a smudge
of menace that draws a line under us all.

Notes to Part One

The Log Delivery: the last line is from the David Bowie song, 'Oh You Pretty Things' "Put another log on the fire for me… Look out my window and what do I see / A crack in the sky and a hand reaching down to me / All the nightmares came today / And it looks as though they're here to stay".

Ynys Enlli: also known as Bardsey Island and is off the coast of the Llyn peninsula in North Wales. It was reputed that 20,000 saints were buried there and it was, and still is, a place of pilgrimage and magic.

The Volta Cinematograph: In 1909 James Joyce was involved in setting up and managing the first dedicated cinema in Ireland. The venture followed sister Eva's comment on the number of cinemas in Trieste compared to the absence of them in Ireland. It never took off and Joyce pulled out quickly from the loss-making venture. The final three lines are broadly Leopold Bloom's from the "Sirens" episode in *Ulysses*.

Supper at Plas-Yn-Rhiw: Plas-Yn-Rhiw is a National Trust property on the Llyn peninsula. It was occupied by the Keating sisters – Eileen, Lorna, Honora – who brought the house back from a parlous state and landscaped the gardens around. The epigram is the sisters' memorial to their parents.

On a Boat with Scully: Dana Scully was a character in *The X-Files*. In an episode in the second series she was in a coma and visualized it as sitting in a boat on a lake deciding whether to return to shore or not. The opening two lines are spoken by Scully in Episode 4, Series 1.

The Politically Incorrect Duck: In 2000, the American Ornithological Union's Committee on Classification and Nomenclature changed the common name of Clangula Hyemalis from Oldsquaw to Long-tailed Duck. Many now refer to it colloquially as the callithumpian duck – the descriptor meaning a noisy celebration using pots and pans banged together.

Pintando Todo El Dia: César Manrique (1919 – 1992) was an artist who devoted himself to ensuring the landscape of Lanzarote was saved from inappropriate tourist development. His diary on display in his studio at his house in Haria has many blank pages with this one sentence at the top – painting all day.

Purusha is a complex Hindu concept. In every Hindu temple is the space for the formless shapeless, all connecting Universal Spirit, the purusha. This space is a small, enclosed, perfect cube, windowless, without ornamentation that represents universal essence.

wonderland: John Atkinson Grimshaw was a Nineteenth Century painter of urban scenes, notably of Leeds.

Light Up Caravaggio: The side altar of the Cesari chapel has a triptych with Carracci's *The Assumption of Mary* in the centre flanked by Caravaggio's *The Conversion of St Paul on the Way to Damascus* and *The Crucifixion of St Peter*.

In An Amount Sufficient to Cause Death: Execution in Arkansas is by intravenous lethal injection; a so-called three-drug protocol administered "in an amount sufficient to cause death". The State announced it would perform eight executions in April 2017 but executed only four prisoners.

Ar Llwybr is the Welsh Coastal Path. The Welsh phrase in the poem means "beware there is danger here".

Hic Omnia Remedia: the Spanish phrase at the end means "shall we start again?".

Fisherman at Laolongtou: the Great Wall of China ends in the Gulf of Bo at Laolongtou. Tong Sui is literally "sugar water" and is a generic sweet dessert in China.

Null Acht Funfzehen: Null-Acht-Funfzehen was the Maxim 08/15 machine gun used by the German army in 1916. The gun fired 500 rounds a minute – one every 0.12 seconds. The opening couplet is translated from the memoirs of Otto Lais, a machine gunner with the German Infantry Regiment 169 at Serre on the first day of the Somme. The phrase is now a German colloquialism meaning something ordinary, unexceptional.

Saturday Market, Rahovec, Kosovo: a qeleshe is a traditional, domed Albanian felt hat, normally white.

— Part Two —

Remarkable Occurrences

This is neither a history, nor a narrative, nor a biography; it is not even a comprehensive survey. It is a sequence of personal reactions in poems, in several voices, to various aspects of Captain James Cook's first voyage in HMB *Endeavour*.

Between 1768 and 1771, Cook circumnavigated the world in a refitted Whitby-built collier, bought by the Royal Navy as the *Earl of Pembroke* but re-named the *Endeavour*. Ostensibly to view the transit of Venus across the Sun from a vantage point in the South Seas, Cook's secret instructions required him to search for a mythical southern continent. In so doing he sailed around and mapped the largely unknown country of New Zealand as well as mapping the west coast of New Holland, now known as Australia. It was probably the greatest feat of seamanship the world had seen since the original navigation from Polynesia of the ancestors of the Maori.

Cook kept a journal of the voyage, published with the sub-title *Remarkable Occurences On His Majesty's Bark Endeavour* (Penguin Edition).

Song of Whitby

This great fisher town
is the start of created things.
First, pure sound, notes
on the stave of Esk, dropping
from the ice-scraped moor,
bucking the trend, heading
no nonsense east straight to the sea
through Whitby's open mouth.

Town of priests and poets,
the river song taken up here.
The first named voice chanting
from Hilda's abbey, singing a song
that sounded across oceans
and seas, an author of miracles.
A sound then rhymed
in oak, canvas, rope, pitch.

The town hymns the world
with the big-bottomed, honest boats
that slip off the banks by the score.
Molto andante, they surge out
over the world's waves.
Rallentando, they return
to the harbour's lop-sided grin,
full of fish, coal, southern pish.

Not this one. The *Earl of Pembroke*
will not return to the white settlement –
this "cat-rigged bark" is navy now.
Two hundred oaks to float a Whitby
collier, they say. Behind this endeavour,
a century of trees, that thrilled to sun
when a king's head was lopped, sail
south, *sostenuto*, to honour one losing his.

Song of the Endeavour

I am *Endeavour*. No more does filthy coal or foul dust choke my hold, clog these decks, this bark now breathes deep and free.

Adieu to "the earl this" or "the lord that", I wear a name proper to the purpose, and will do my duty.

Bluff-bowed and blunt – a hopper-arsed and tumblehome craft – but at my heart beats northern oak.

Look you well on Cook's favoured tool to jemmy open the sea's secrets. No ship of fools but an ark of talents:

charters of continents fill my cabins – arts and sciences wed to realise the expectations of the age…to know, to take, to have.

Still a clumsy, shallow wooden box you laugh; maybe once, but reborn cheeky and bold to defy all wrecking seas.

No figurehead to see for'ard, calm the deep; yet, brave sailors, do not fear, for I will caper cat-pawed and loose-jointed over all waves,

spooling out lines to snag new lands, draw them out of empty ocean. Here is the chosen instrument of a King's will: I am *Endeavour*.

Song of George Dorlton

I was his shadow, close, opaque;
his mirror too, flaunting the pale face
of better. With me, he shone radiantly;
his ascension was my eclipse.
A servant-slave, living in his pockets,
strutting the streets, acting the gentleman.
Never the mungo, never sulky, I ate
from his table, slept in his beds,
wore his clothes, all with a frozen grin.
I was comfortable – but a silver collar
chafes worse than any iron one.

Now laid out in snow, a shade cast
by no man. I am stolen, lost to myself,
now abandoned. Another swig of rum
warms briefly, like the ripening sun,
better than the ruby-red sweat of my yoked
brothers and sisters that I have drunk.
This land of fire shrouds me with wintry ash.
My bleached bones will layer with snow,
hard frost will make an icy cairn of me.
I am dying, nothing remarkable in that.
I take hold of the darkness… damn them all…

Song of the Young Sailor

1

All this voyage, the fear, scraping away,
digging deep; work is a sanative routine
but always the Tars are at it – shipworms
boring in, hollowing out, until their words
echo and echo in my head.'*Tis a four square
world; elemental, no–one can live southwards.
Damnation awaits if we sail over the edge.
They lay out proofs as if enlightened men.
Tell me, where are the four corners of a ball?
Are we heathens? A round earth contradicts
Scripture. How can antipodes see Christ's
second coming with feet above their heads?*

2

All was contention in me until Tahiti; the joys
of Venus careened minds of idle thoughts.
Then the secret was out: Earth is a sphere
and we must pursue new lands, the equipoisure.
Terra Australis Nondum Cognita is the goal!
We chase the counterweight that keeps
this ball whirling safe in the heavens.
There were always portents, but hanging cloud
or thick horizons don't make a landfall.
Simple men will seize on anything that points
to the grand object they covet. Then, young Nick
shouts, the tip of the great continent is ours.

3

April and we leave these fogged islands.
The continent-mongers are quieted, conned
by this New Zealand – the consolation prize,
now well-charted but not much better known.
Each day we have sailed increases our knowledge
and deepens our ignorance too. But the problem
is never what we don't know; it is what we think
we know, that experience will prove wrong.
The old sailors start up again – *no continent, no ballast!*
The earth will roll us off – now a childish argument.
We are all changed; either here or nowhere –
all is mystery. It matters not – we know the sea.

Song of William Greenslade, Marine

Here, I crave those purging moments
when I hang between past and future.
The cold scraping air will rasp me clean;
a scaled fish leaping back to the water.

My Sunday devotions this holy day –
to step from the ship in prayer,
shriven spotless. No stain of thief,
no William Greenslade, no Marine;

not striped, not broken – all sloughed off.
My service is over, sin is pardoned;
again a raw lad who watched soldiers drill.
Still my duty must be done. Sentinel

at the steerage door, a soldier boy,
alone as always on this passage.
Baited and bullied by my comrades,
an outcast shunned or mocked.

In my pocket is the mark of my sin –
a sealskin patch, stolen for a purse,
smaller than my palm it drags me down.
I will be made to pay in full for my shame.

They say land is near but no honour
comes of desertion, a life with heathens.
Soon enough I will take my ease,
offer myself for the voyage's good luck,

stride out from the forecastle into the water,
dazzling as ice. I will float in my purgatory
long enough to watch my life fade into shadow.
Not lost overboard but found again.

And all that remains is the limitless sea.

Song of Joseph Banks

Orion rises up topsy-turvy
in the blackest of nights.
As I lie down to sleep,
all is perplexity here;
a country so new to the eyes,
that sight itself must be forgotten
and relearned to welcome
the infinite variety of creation.
Mrs Endeavour gives us a true arcadia
where we become kings of curiosity.

We are enlightened in our ignorance.
We make maps as we go.
What we know is always behind us,
the future an intimation only; hints,
as twigs and grasses on a current
or bands of soft light on a coloured sea,
suggest.

I have woken here to birds, enchanted
by their melodious wild music.
I hear the song – a silver wind
in the tree line – but my business
on this voyage is to kill variety,
to make specimen of all that present.
The learned society of the great cabin
has shot, trapped, hooked, netted, picked
the abundance of this land.
I have eaten my way through the bounty
of this paradise further than any man; fortune
has brought us here but we may leave
cornucopia a mere hollowed horn.

There were ten thousand reasons
for coming and when I leave
there will be many thousands more to go home –
in preserving jar, boxes, sketch books, plant pots.
Bone, beak, feather, seed –
the residue of all that I have seen,
now shriveled, dried out husks of memory.
They will adorn lecture or dinner party;
all will marvel, presented with the telescope of my journey,
but all must view from the wrong end:
remarkable wonders, far off, foreshortened, stunted.

This land unlearns us.
We are rational men, free-thinkers
who would clear our minds
absorb multitudes –
but what language does this land speak
that we can comprehend?
Beached, in the dark,
all is whisper and circumlocution;
shore, sound, forest and river mouth
declare themselves only to confound.

We travel but are not travellers
for whom the journey is ample warrant.
This is no voyage of mere curiosity.
We are explorers: God's organisers,
proceeding categorically
by inquiry and investigation,
we impose order.

Here is a new Adam to whom birds
fly, plants lean, fish swim,
unknowing and unsuspicious,
to be taken, named, taxonomised.

Song of Tupaia

He is the traveller; the internationalist,
moving over the centuries' diaspora
in his righteous knowledge. A map?
He'll speak of hundreds of islands
within a radius of two thousand miles,
and name half of them for you, too.

A sniff of wind, the swell of a wave
a seabird's wing catching the sun –
he knows where, in this consanguine
ocean, the ship lies; and always, always,
the direction from which Tahiti invites.
He is savvy. Schooled in wisdom, stories

where ancestors sang to him of paths
in the stars, swore to sail side by side forever.
He is the god carrier, the tattoo wearer,
the saviour of the royal red feather girdle.
Tupaia, the wayfinder priest – ingenious,
shrewd – who knows which way the wind

blows even before it puffs up the sails.
He wears this know-how lightly – a sacred
cloak that becomes him, it is woven in,
dyed into his fabric. Organic.
No need to extort homage; he is sacred,
a sage, an initiator into rituals, into lore.

This is not science; some on the ship reckon
it, follow instructions, go their own way,
confident in their calculations and brass,
their shipboard routines and almanacs.
Tupaia who gave them the South Sea Islands
is supernumary, a token experimental gentleman.

Positively haughty, wanting the deference
due an *arioi*; but there is no free-born Jack
who will lightly bend the knee to an Indian.
Tupaia is aloof, not beaten; he has set forth
as a seed and knows he will flourish.
In New Zealand he becomes the mediator,

the emollient, the resolver of perplexity.
He is the leader here; his words speak
to all. He swims amongst the tribes
like a blessed fish returned to the gods.
The Maoris welcome Tupaia – a dog-skin
cloak for the *Tohunga* who fulfills prophecy,

who comes from the inherited homeland
like 'Oro himself with thunder and death.
His legend travels up the coast, smoke
in the wind – the canoes come out in finery,
to parley with this emissary out of the horizon;
the chiefs in their red and ochre are amazed.

Nothing lasts. Farewell and Tupaia's stars
are occluded, the way is unclear, his words
unheard. Once some were curious of him,
now he is a curiosity that might prove cheap
to keep, whose cheeping might entertain
for a season, the salons and houses of England.

But Tupaia is dying. He will never see England
nor his home again. All must suffer one day
but not now, not here. Take him to the shore,
let him face the ocean, let his spirit flow free.
Who sings for you, Tupaia? Who dances for you?
Where are you going, Tupiaa…

Seaward…
departed, dead, alas Tupaia…

Song of Young Nick

This morning all was beyond me.
Look up from below deck,
I could see each rung that may
lift me to an Admiral's pomp.
A cabin boy is servant to all
but the future is his to dream.
I climb the rigging, all changes;
down there this wooden world
shrinks, is flattened out, abridged.

At the masthead my creation
is limitless and liminal. I dangle
between sea and sky; all is prospect.
I become the gentle breezes
that unspin me, empty me out;
I am the flowing sea unwinding
me to the horizon, that fluid frame
of all and nothing. Everything
let go, voided, naught yet grasped.

I am the eye that comprehends all;
rightly I see the suggestion of land,
a smudge edging knowledge. No age,
but my name defines this discovery.
Now the gentlemen regale themselves;
laugh that *terra australis* is now *cognita*.
They will map, collect, classify, only
my soul will keep pure a child-imagined
land, tainted by our uncertain steps.

Song of the Kauri Trees

We were gods without parents;
lords of the forest
who parted earth and sky.
We held in creels of leaf and twig
the memory of how all might fit,
if the words – hardly known –
were spoken right.
We were the world completed;
neither seeing nor being seen,
the beginning and the end.
Whisperers of the things unknown,
that danced at the edge of sense.

Time wasn't.
Only the rituals of tide,
the ebb and flow incantation of sea.
No ghosts to stir the bark-flaked trails.
No-one to swim as fish through the ferns,
until the ordinary people happened.
In myth from the start,
loosed on the ocean in song,
they unmade themselves.
Carved canoes became them;
delivered them
like the emptying of a holey kitbag
that leaked light
among us black trees.
Bound together between shadows
our sharing is magic.

We are nobility in Aotearoa.
In sacred spaces we are carved
immortal; gave back faces
that laugh out the inner life.
We stood together and belonged;
here and now, here was connection.
We are the chief and we are the log
launched on the final journey home.

Time was.
A calculus of curiosity brought it here,
where epoch and era were the only true measures,
not the trivial dicing of day and night.
Three sparse, shrouded trunks –
aloft of a basket of wood –
made a stand in the bay,
hauled the horizon
as close to this coastline as reason allowed.
Emptied on shore were creatures,
as if a flock of birds,
who sized up land, river and forest,
named things already known.
Markers of the hours,
who could not foretell this bounty.
Here was an auspicious future
to be sniffed at, possessed.

We were surveyed, charted, logged;
taken out of ourselves,
put on the map for all to see.
But we were diminished;
made landscape by this landing.
We became assets; admirable timber,
great ghosts of the forests,
already shrinking from this island.
The world was restored
but we were scarred to the bark.
Lightning struck the mountains,
rain flooded the rivers; the great wind
returned between land and sky.
All shivered, mastered by those
who have set the sun,
placed the moon at a distance,
will inevitably return to a land now theirs.

Song of the First Contact

Look,
this is the scene:
the bay is empty, then,
it is full.
A new island floats,
or, a bird – giant,
feathered – lands.
No-one saw it coming;
but maybe there was a warning,
some recall a prophecy
of strangers,
a time of darkness.
Is this imagined?
No, canoes landed
here long ago;
people arrive to make
this land theirs,
even gods might come.

I come, and an unknown earth lies below my feet.

Astonishment and fear;
people are sick.
Best to turn away,
ignore it. That's impossible:
now there are fledglings,
no feathers, many legs,
in the water of the bay.
Bright colours, plumage,
in human shapes;
backwards, they come on
blindly backwards.

It is no island, no bird;
it is His Majesty's Bark.
Smoke rises at the tree line.
They must land here:
fresh water to find,
discoveries to make.
Swivel guns are fixed up,
men busy themselves,
eager to explore;
they have been here before.
Pinnace and yawl launch,
row shoreward,
now observed.

Canoes are beached,
the people gather
but things seem out of kilter,
as if time has slipped,
a microsecond displacement.
Nothing makes sense.
Waves lap the sand
but speak differently;
maybe ears are not working,
or sounds are slipping
under the waves.
There is puzzlement.

The god/humans open their mouths
but nothing can be heard.
They are in the river,
they are on the shore,
they are near the huts.

Te Maro and some warriors
know what to do,
but the canoe bird
slips away; they follow.
The thunder stops them solid
but nothing to see;
the men go on.
Thunder again;
Te Maro raises a spear
in guarded welcome.
A stick is raised back;
it roars, he falls
to the sand, still.
Why is he lying still,
no-one has struck at him.
He is dragged away,
he cannot move.
He has become sacred
and should be left;
he should be covered.

I come and a new heaven turns above me.

The land is clean again;
only the tribes live here tonight,
though some are dead.
Many people sit deliberating;
what is happening,
what is to be done,
better for all if these gods leave.

The ship will not leave.
There are instructions –
natives are to be observed,
things must be understood,
ordered,
contact must be made.
Come morning all boats land;
some friendship is cultivated,
exchanges of words and gifts
but the day turns disagreeable,
wry faces are made
eyes are rolled, tongues poked;
the marines are called.

Many more have landed,
walking in a line
holding the sticks
that kill with breath.
It is important to know
if they come in peace;
they must know
the people's steadfastness,
the strength of their arms.
The warriors challenge them –
it is their territory;
they are answered
with thunder that stirs the waters.
Te Rakau must seize a weapon

but is punished immediately,
shot dead maybe,
others wounded.
It should not be like this.
They have shown them iron,
shown presents of beads, nails;
have told them they are friends,
here to trade,
to collect water and wood
but they cannot be stung with spears
or knocked on the head.
They cannot have weapons
snatched away.
It is hard to understand
if you were not there,
on the precarious brink
of everything known.
They must defend themselves,
they must say, watch us,
we are strong, we are dangerous,
but we can be friendly;

they smile and call to the fishermen
whose canoes cross the bay,
who cannot flee,
who are afraid
who fight with paddles and stones
who are shot dead.
It is justifiable;
they are understanding the people better.

They couldn't let them escape
to demonstrate their bravery,
to weaken the King's power.
All are on the edge of the world here,
care must be taken

especially of the three children,
scared of being killed and eaten,
who, while companions die,
jump off the canoe
are netted and brought aboard
to be made friends.
These boys are fed, beds made for them
presents given to them.
These gods are not frightening
their food is plentiful
their drinks refreshing.
One talks their language
and in the dark night of fear
before the boys are restored,
sings with them songs,
like psalms, of the tribes,
of the ancestors.

I come on to this earth and it is a peaceful resting-place for me.

There is nothing to be got from here;
no trade, no water,
only ducks shot, wood cut.
It was not supposed to be like this.

There is regret at the killings
but the dead remain dead;
the living show no fear
of the muskets leveled at them.
They gather again
with spears and clubs;
the tribes will defend what is theirs.
Why is this not understood?

This is Poverty Bay.
There is nothing useful here;
little to gain. Forty plant specimens
boxed, recorded; the land noted,
measured out, absorbed.
There is nothing useful here.
The ship will sail on.

Now it is morning again.
The bay is empty;
there is birdsong, waves are heard,
the huts chatter and buzz.
There are rituals to be done.
It is Turanga nui a Kiwa.
All is restored,
the people breathe out.
Everything is the same
with the gods gone…

everything is changed.

O spirit of the planets!
The stranger humbly offers you his heart as nourishment.

Song of Sydney Parkinson

This cabin is a coffin shared
with a curious land's dead flora
and fauna, that my inks
and watercolours work to resurrect
for all at home to see. Each day

the lines at the horizon have resolved
into the crumpled paper of landscape
which I must smooth and fill feverishly
with proof of all the wonders we see.
None will comprehend God's diverse

marvels except through my eyes, the skill
of my hands. It is a heavy burden;
my obligation is no more to art,
only learning. I am a recorder,
a documentary painter who proves

we are not mere collecting macaronis,
but men of science, enlightened men.
I have tried to free my mind of convention,
to express these wonders in a new way
of seeing that puts the viewer on the spot,

to witness how these places smelled,
sounded, felt, of how the light
made sea and land dissolve in itself,
of how these peoples lived and breathed,
were more than exhibits, exemplars

of exotic types. But it is too much.
This second paradise offers up subjects
so rapidly that colour itself must only
be noted in a cursory manner, as if others
are destined to complete my work.

Though the work calms me, as nightly
I dream Buchan, sewn in a sheet slipping
easily from the pinnace into the peace
of the bay; only his drawings linger
to tell of him. I redouble my efforts.

Now this botanical draughtsman,
whose delight is forever natural history,
must capture everything; against time,
against the peculiar putrescent quality
of the very air that rots away flesh

while I sketch and dab under a net.
It is easier here to catch fish without
a hook than it is to draw them, in rivalry
with insect and maggot. A feather fly-flap
more beneficial than a paintbrush!

I work by candle or moon, so silently
that the din of grasshoppers stuns me.
These lands have left their mark on me;
as the scrape of nib, the daub of paint
imprint their mark on my paper. Indelible.

It is enough to make a man quake.

Song of the Tupapaku

There is a seal in the bay, or,
there is a mermaid in the bay.
You may believe anything here,
when even the light of reason dims.

A body, female, unbound, bellying
in the swell. Well, we are told
there are no graves here;
no pomposity of ceremony.

Death is a secret place;
a corpse tethered to a stone
splashes into the bay's depths,
that might be it for eternity.

An image is disconcerting me:
the seabed of the bay, and beyond,
gravid with the weighted dead
pinned like underwater kites.

All float upright, roped by ankle;
all look seaward, vibrating
imperceptibly in the slack water
as if tuned to a higher wavelength.

Nervous, they flutter, shy virgins
on the edge, hoping to dance
a slow undersea cotillion.
Waiting for partners... waiting for us.

Song of the Cannibalism

Here is the black heart
of this new world.
There can be no surprise;
no need for any grinning
farce, for this gumming
of fleshy forearm.
The evidence is clear,
any sceptic is persuaded.
There lie the bones,
picked clean of dainty bits,
gnawed and tooth-marked.

All know that extremity
will drive anyone to survive –
pricked by the goad of necessity
who would not fall away
from the civilised state?
But this devilish communion
is beyond the pale of expedience.
It is pleasing that observation
can confirm speculation;
though these wily people
may yet have made a joke of us.

Here, we are marginal men,
peripheral to everything.
In our voyeuristic amity
with these denizens,
we may see ourselves
as in a distorting mirror.
In knowing these natives,
we might understand
ourselves the better;
but, even so, we will never
gauge which is truly the other.

Song of the Severed Head

A severed head is just that,
no more nor no less disengaged
than you would expect
of a hairy scalp, a face of skin,
a bone box cluttered now with flax.
A bargain made at musket point;
for one who will no more wonder
at the stars seen from a canoe,
who will not again see sunrise
over sea, nor speak of mysteries
in savage, moon-bathed, symposiums.
Such sentimentality! Better suited
to romantic notions, I fear.
Yet this new world is inscrutable,
its sublime novelties assail us daily,
and might leave us, like you now,
blind, mute, fumbling to comprehend it;
might render these overburdened brains
unable to fashion a logical account.
No! Reason is always the key.
We are ingenious men, logical,
clear-headed not starry-eyed.
Our science will improve man's estate;
yours was no more than ingenuity,
enough to get by in this far corner
until we exposed the world outside.
It is us who crossed oceans, you,
worth a pair of old linen drawers,
must swing carelessly in my cabin.

The Song of Possession

Near Fools' holy day and what we think we've
seen slides away into rain and cloud,
as if it never existed. Perhaps it never did.
Nothing can be trusted to memory alone.
The islands diminish slowly into mist, are gone.
This part of the job is finished, only recalled
like the seawaters that pass under the keel.
Though lead, latitude and lookout served well,
all is contingent as the continent disappears.
At least Tasman's sketchy question mark
has an answer; we have mapped,
measured and charted these islands;
now they lie differently from before.
We have enlightened them, taken possession.
The land is pinioned with flagpoles, colours
flap to the air, names and dates carved
on trees. A King, losing a new world,
has acquired the promise of a newer one.
These islands are weighted down; a warranty
against their slipping away for ever.
Pyramids of stone, salted with musket balls,
shot beads, loose change – whatever will stand
the test of time – proclaim to latecomers, "look,
we were here, it's ours". A flag unfurled,
a King's health toasted in blood-red wine,
the empty bottle presented to an old man
who seems delighted. This is the way: we trade
whimsies for intercourse and curiosities.
We give trifles to these noble and raw-boned people;
they have given us dominion over them.

Song of the Leaving

No farewells from the cape
that day; resolved to quit
the country altogether,
they steer westward,
where the sun vanishes.

No glances backwards;
once more, all they are
is contained by the ship,
until fancy may encounter
further, unknown shores.

They came as goblins,
tricky and dangerous,
manageable with care.
Go as ghosts, blurry, faint
in the mist. Unknowable.

Ten tall forest trees fallen;
no need for dirges to chant
the ship's passing away.
No more breath to be shared
with these spirit people

Te Ika a Māui, Te Wāhi
Pounamu are; life resumes.
Some left might ponder
on new worlds revealed
by the might-be gods.

Others may have held
a nail, examined a cairn
of stones, wondered
which tribe the visitors
claimed kinship with.

Crew and tribes settle back
into routine rhythms.
They have swapped much,
though the final gift
exposed remains unnamed.

Song of Botany Bay

("The sea carried this ship here, why?")

Those who watched were right
to be anxious. Caretakers
of this country for ever, deep time
guardians of the sacred white clay,
inhabitants of an old story, not living
simply but living complex in spirit
and communion maintained
from the first day, they could not see
the portent standing up out of the bay.
It was no whale blowing,
no dream time coming of plenty –
these figures rowing ashore were not gods,
maybe song men and sorcerers,
maybe white-skinned ancestor spirits;
who knows anything, except they came
without consent, without ceremony,
without essence.

Two men – marked and pierced,
befitting those who know, who understand –
went forward with spears and shields,
obligated to protect their country
to find the ritual which affirms
to strangers they are Gweagal,
who belong with the land, its plenty,
always have, always will.
It is them,
it is theirs.
The others do not see things like that.
They discover Botany Bay,
see nothing extraordinary, a few
bark huts, women not giving a fig
for decency, natives waving spears,
advancing to combat.

Shots are fired and two retreat,
one injured. The clan draws back
observes; the strangers know nothing,
have no stories, have no dreams.
They cannot speak the animals, the plants.
They don't even know the names of here;
why they have come isn't clear. Ignore them.
They take spears and shields, offer nothing
back of any import – beads, a dead bird, nails.
Some new things in the world,
but useless things that may be cursed,
stuff not to be dreamt of by a nation
of philosophers who know how many things
there are that they don't want.
Maybe everything should be thrown
into the sea.

The strangers survey and measure up
an empty topography as if it is new,
a void needing filling, but it's layered
with spirit and meaning – nuanced, timeless –
where people walk with ancestors
across this created, singing landscape.
Always was, always will be, they think…
A week under the Jack is only
the beginning. This is *terra nullius,*
a land that starts this day,
that is potential now, not past – 65,000
years means nothing.
No-one has the right to occupy a country
without voluntary consent –
their orders said that –
but this is different.

It is a blank land; a new Eden
if emptied of its Adam and Eve.
We can admire them for their ignorant
happiness, their absence of acquisitiveness –
but they don't own this place.
They don't labour, they don't plough, they don't sow;
they cannot reap. The Crown can possess
this land, all will benefit.
Except the custodians, who are footnotes
in a new history of Australia.
Identity goes along with the land – the clans
become aboriginals. In this great growing silence,
the people, who can only beat the ground
with their fists, wonder why the sea
carried this ship to this place;
what will it mean?

Song of the Bitch, Lady

The bitch, Lady, is dead; in sight
of home she is the final fatality.
One gull-shriek in the night
and that was that, end of the trip.
One howl and the past three years
becomes memory. She is stiffening
on the stool, still guarding the table
where Banks wrote the journal
that mentioned her only in death.
He seemed surprised, as if, despite
the late voyage carnage, nothing
more of his should be taken.

Now the world will be Banks' bitch;
that trots dutifully, wherever he leads,
that eagerly laps up what he puts down.

Song of Celebrity

When eagle-eyed Nick saw the Lizard,
it was all over bar the shouting.
The seafarers left the circled globe behind
to nuzzle up to a bigger world: London.
They land in Kent, already become famous –
survivors are superstars. Gossip sheets, agog
with letters that outpaced the tired bark,
make it up. Fake news! A numbers game
of marvels: a million specimens, new plants
aplenty, strange creatures, stranger peoples,
a southern continent disgorging bounty
for all! And here is a poster boy for a counterfeit
cruise – rich, young, toothsome, Joseph Banks,
bigged-up – *immortalis* – a man without equals,
daubed on canvas, lauded, doctorated,
courted by a curious king who adds him
to the growing queue. See his name
in lights above the titles, starring with sociable
Dan Solander in their own buddy movie–
"The Return of the Ingenious Gentlemen".
Thus is this voyage inflated; in its puffery
becoming something much less than it was.
What did it achieve? The special day for
astronomers when Venus transited spoiled
by a dusty penumbra. No southern continent –
though the Captain was right to resist
any blame laid to his charge. What else
might contribute to the success of the venture:
more than many insects of course, the curiosities,
the illustrations – these might resurrect it.

But they are like fish out of water losing
the dazzle of scale, the verve of a piercing eye;
like birds taken out of the air, become leaden,
drab. All can be pored over, spiked, buried
in dusty drawers, bound in heavy volumes,
folded into paper shrouds – forgotten until
a florilegium rebirth. But no tally sheet
is needed; no apologies necessary.
Achievements? Enough that it was.
There's no sentiment in this navy anyhow.
The hero bark is soon a shuttling Falkland
transport, scuttled quickly enough in the service
of empire. A little R & R and sailors sign on
for more service. Officers take new orders;
ambition awaits the next war. The captain
himself will go again, in the end lose it
chasing another imperial chimera.
There is a tide in celebrity too,
that rolls back and leaves the beached
icon's wax wings to melt in the sunshine.
Even the great self-promoter plays his cards
badly: hubris demands Banks is thrown off
the next voyage. The vultures circle:
the fop becomes a fly-catching macaroni,
an alligator-eater, the South Sea
caterpillar transformed into a Bath butterfly.
Worse, the celeb becomes a sexual tourist,
losing his trousers to a dusky, exotic queen,
inviting play with his proboscis, smiling
without pleasantry, wenching without passion.

All things must pass. The voyage fades, lapses,
is an apologue. What yesterday was vital,
vivacious, wilts to reminiscence, losing definition
and proportion, but still evoked endlessly
in lecture-hall, around dining tables
where airy dreams might entertain friends
(if only Buchan had lived!).
Tars too, below decks, in dark, smoky
dockside inns, recount tales of the South Seas,
taller, more lubricious with each repetition.
Once everything was theirs to know –
alluring, glittering, imprinted
on eye and mind, outstripping imagination,
infinite possibility opening up daily
under the quickening prow. Each league
sailed changed them, transmuted them.
Every crew member carries close
to his heart a relic of the true voyage;
intense of colour, of sound, of smell,
of feel. The moments of exultation,
despair, rank fear; sadness and loss too;
that late cull reminding all that death
owns them and when death calls
they may hope to pray on that relic
one last time and, for a shining moment,
to be back with *Endeavour*.
A full crew under blue skies; the comfort
of a ship that does as it is asked;
a fresh wind, a healthy swell rolling
them onward to the southern ocean,
into the unknown… forever.

Notes to Remarkable Occurences

Song of Whitby: The italicized words are musical terms. *Andante* means moderately slow; *rallentando* means gradually getting slower; *sostenuto* means sustained.

Song of the Endeavour: the Endeavour was, technically, a bark with features such as a lack of figurehead

Song of George Dorlton: George Dorlton was one of two servants of African descent taken on the voyage by Joseph Banks. Black servants were popular with the English aristocracy at the time. Dorlton also assisted as a field collector of specimens. Both servants died of hypothermia on Tierra Del Fuego when caught out at night in an unexpected snowstorm.

Song of the Young Sailor: several of the crew were young men, almost children, starting out on a maritime career. *Terra Australis Nondum Cognita* means "the southern land not yet known" – one of the descriptors of the anticipated great southern continent which was thought to balance off the known lands north of the Equator and which often appeared in old maps. The word "equipoisure" is that of the 18th century French scholar Charles De Broses. Cook's secret instructions, opened after Tahiti, were to find the continent.

Song of William Greenslade, Marine: Greenslade was a Private in the Marine detachment of twelve. In March 1769 he was thought to have stolen a piece of seal's skin, used for tobacco pouches, and reported to the Sergeant of Marines. It was thought that, filled with shame, he jumped overboard and was drowned in the Pacific. One explanation is that his mind was affected by scurvy.

Song of Joseph Banks: Sir Joseph Banks was an aristocratic naturalist, botanist and scientist and later a controversial President of the Royal Society of London for Improving Natural Knowledge. He paid for himself (£10,000, worth not far off £1.5 million today) and a team of scientists and illustrators to accompany Cook on his first voyage.

Song of Tupaia: Tupaia was from the island of Raiatea but joined the voyage at Tahiti and was intending to visit England. He was a high priest, aristocrat and member of a cult – the 'Arioi dedicated to 'Oro the god of war. He was a skilled navigator and linguist and was understood in New Zealand and treated as a high status visitor – as such he acted as an intermediary between the ship and the Maori and helped gloss over various breaches of local etiquette and ritual. He died of fever in Batavia on the return leg though his use to the ship after New Zealand was limited as he could not communicate with the aboriginal people of Australia and became increasingly withdrawn and ill. Tohunga literally means "chosen", experts in a particular activity. The last line was reputedly the song of the people of Tolaga Bay in 1773 having heard of the death of Tupiaia.

Song of Young Nick: Young was eleven years old when the *Endeavour* left England 1768. He was the personal servant of the surgeon, William Monkhouse. He won a reward of rum for being the first to spot land (New Zealand) on October 1769. Cook named Young Nick's Head near Poverty Bay after him. Young first spotted the Lizard Head on the return to England.

Song of the Kauri Trees: Kauri were ancient trees which could live to a 1,000 years old. They were important in Maori stories and mythology. Europeans prized the wood for shipbuilding and construction and, eventually, the forests were extensively logged. Aotearoa became the accepted Maori name for New Zealand.

Song of the First Contact: Cook's first contact with Maori was disastrous with several shot dead and no meaningful communication over the two and a half days the *Endeavour* stayed in what Cook called Poverty Bay, now named Turanga nui a Kiwa Poverty Bay. The italicized lines are from a Maori prayer centred on the God Pourangahua who was brought to New Zealand by a silver firebird that scorched the land.

Song of Sydney Parkinson: Sydney Parkinson was employed for £80 per annum by Joseph Banks as a botanical draughtsman tasked with drawing specimens but took over Alexander Buchan's work on landscape drawing when Buchan died in Tahiti. Parkinson himself died after falling ill on the way home and was buried at sea – the Log

Book recording him as "DD" (discharged dead) and hundreds of his sketches were later completed by watercolourists hired by Banks.

Song of the Tūpāpaku: the word is a Maori word meaning deceased or corpse. Joseph Banks reported that Maori dead were not buried but tied to a stone and put into the sea.

Song of the Cannibalism: The expedition was obsessed with the possibility of cannibalism in New Zealand and received several indications that it was not uncommon.

Song of the Severed Head: In 1770 Joseph Banks purchased a preserved tattooed head from an elderly Maori in Queen Charlotte Sound. The man took the price, as Banks wrote, of "a pair of old drawers of very white linen."

Song of Possession: The *Endeavour* left New Zealand on March 31st/April 1st, 1770 having formally possessed the land for King George III.

Song of the Leaving: Te Ika a Māui and Te Wāhi Pounamu translate as, respectively, The Fish of Maui and The Place of Greenstone and were Maori names for the North Island and the South Island of the current New Zealand.

Song of Botany Bay: The epigram comes from a response to seeing Endeavour offshore – " Must be songmen and sorcerers…The sea carried this ship here, why?" The Gweagal were a clan of the Eora tribe of Indigenous Australians who are traditional custodians of the area around Sydney including what Cook called Botany Bay. Benjamin Franklin, after hearing the story of the Gweagal disinterest in the baubles left described them as a nation of philosophers and envied their awareness of all the things in the world they did not want. The description *Terra Nullius*, literally "nobody's land" with its rejection of the 65,000 year long occupation by the indigenous people, is seen by some as the justification for claiming Australia.

Song of the Bitch, Lady: Lady was one of Joseph Banks' dogs on the voyage. She was the last fatality on the voyage.

Song of Celebrity: The aristocratic, young and rich Joseph Banks especially became a celebrity. But the papers/satirists rounded on him and focused on his sexual tourism, heedless consumption of the world, the airy-fairy approach to science of a specimen collector. Boswell described Banks as "an elephant, quite placid and gentle, allowing you to get on his back and play with his proboscis". When Dr Johnson suggested the voyagers had found very little, Boswell replied "but many insects, Sir". The *Florilegium* was intended to collect in one publication all of the specimen illustrations associated with the *Endeavour* voyage. It was never published in Banks' lifetime. The first complete full-colour edition of the *Florilegium* was published in a limited edition between 1980 and 1990.